C ᵜᴗᴿᴿ

A Case of Obscurity
in Accomplishment

David N. Thomas

COMMUNITY DEVELOPMENT FOUNDATION
• PUBLICATIONS •

First published in Great Britain in 1995 by
Community Development Foundation
60 Highbury Grove
London N5 2AG

The right of David N. Thomas to be identified as author of this work has been asserted by him in accordance with the *Copyright Designs and Patents Act* 1988.

Cover design by Edward Bear Associates, Amsterdam
Typeset by Stanford Desktop Publishing Services, Milton Keynes
Printed in Great Britain

British Library Cataloguing-in-Publication Data
A record of this publication is available from the British Library.

ISBN 0 902406 95 7

The *Joseph Rowntree Foundation* has supported this project as part of its programme of research and innovative development projects, which it hopes will be of value to policy-makers and practitioners. The facts presented and the views expressed are those of the authors and not necessarily those of the Foundation.

Community Development Foundation

The Community Development Foundation (CDF) was set up in 1968 to pioneer new forms of community development.

CDF strengthens communities by ensuring the effective participation of people in determining the conditions which affect their lives. It does this through:

* providing support for community initiatives
* promoting best practice
* informing policy-makers at local and national level.

As a leading authority on community development in the UK and Europe, CDF is a non-departmental public body and is supported by the Voluntary Services Unit of the Home Office. It receives substantial backing from local and central government, trusts and business.

CDF promotes community development through:

* local action projects
* conferences and seminars
* consultancies and training programmes
* research and evaluation services
* parliamentary and public policy analysis
* information services
* *CDF News*, a quarterly newsletter
* publications.

Chairman: Alan Haselhurst, MP
Chief Executive: Alison West

Community Development Foundation
60 Highbury Grove
London N5 2AG
Tel: 0171 226 5375
Fax: 0171 704 0313
Registered Charity Number 306130

FALL

One day you look up, and the leaves are falling,
Already lying thick along the paths –
They wheeze when stepped on, like a posthumous breath
In which you seem to hear a whispered message;
For all the while your thoughts were busy elsewhere
They dutifully, one by one, slipped off,
Withdrawing quietly from the congregation.
Some fell on stony ground or at the roadside,
And every time a lorry hurried past
A few stood up and tried to totter after,
Then sank again like uncomplaining derelicts.
Some fell among the brambles and were choked.
Some stayed beneath their oak and faithfully
Reflected back the russet like a pool.
Others fell on good ground, and though themselves
Not fruitful, gave their wealth for seeds
To flourish and yield fruit. So what's the message?
Don't ask me; I might be tempted to project
My self-reproach for failures of attention,
And my chagrin at vain or early deaths.

Stevie Krayer

Contents

Acknowledgements

I owe much to Alan Haselhurst, MP, Chairman of the Community Development Foundation, and to his fellow Trustees. They provided support and encouragement, and were generous with their advice and insight.

The work for this report, and the larger study on which it is based, was possible because of the assistance and interest of the Joseph Rowntree Foundation. I am grateful to its Trustees for their help.

I am indebted to those who read and commented on my drafts: Gabriel Chanan, Ross Flockhart, Paul Henderson, David Jones, Pat Kneen, Stevie Krayer, Walter James, Janet Novak, Jerry Smith and Alison West. Thanks, too, to those who spoke with me about CDF and community development, or who corresponded with me, including a good number of former and present CDF staff and Trustees. Dorrett Crooks, Kevin Harris, Catriona May and Pauline Gaskill provided me with excellent back-up support.

Above all, my further thanks to Gabriel, Paul and Stevie, whose ideas and care (for both communities and writing), are to be found in this report.

David Thomas
Ciliau Aeron
Lampeter

Introduction

This report is about community development, and draws largely on my experience whilst Chief Executive of the Community Development Foundation (CDF). The report discusses some of the lessons from the work of CDF, within the context of wider events in community development in Britain and other parts of Europe.

I suggest that community development has been distorted by the short-term needs of policy-makers; it has been used more as an 'alternative' solution to dealing with residual problems in society and the economy, rather than as a way of enhancing social processes within communities. The development of communities has not been sufficiently recognised as a good, and as a goal, in its own right. Problem-solving community projects have taken the place of, rather than being used as part of, a longer-term process of capacity-building in local communities. Moreover, community workers themselves have largely been concerned only with the *crisis of poverty* in communities; they have mostly ignored the *crisis of belonging and identity*, or thought naïvely that it would be solved as a by product of dealing with poverty.

The report begins with a a brief review of some of the wider factors affecting community development in the 1980s, and then presents data from CDF field projects as a way of highlighting the extent of *community interaction* to be found in even the most deprived urban neighbourhoods. Much, though not all, of this interaction is cooperative; that is, it involves people working with each other to achieve common goals in and for their locality.

Section 3 builds upon the work of a number of authors, including Chanan's important research on the community sector (1992). I try to suggest ways that social processes within communities can be identified at the heart of community development.

In section 4, I criticise the lack of clarity about tasks, and outcomes in community projects, and suggest ways that much of the work of community projects can be evaluated using quantitative measures. This chapter includes some material on the impact of CDF field work at local and national levels.

The last section contains a brief appraisal of the lessons to be learnt from CDF's fieldwork, as well as an assessment of the contribution of community's development.

Finally, this present report is distilled from a more detailed account of the work of CDF, to be published in late 1995 and available from CDF Publications. The fuller account will contain further elaboration of some of the material in this report, as well as two case studies; one of these case studies deals with the setting up of CDF in 1968, and the other with the events surrounding the negotiations in the late 1980s between the Calouste Gulbenkian Foundation and CDF about the latter's role as a national body for community development.

1   Mission Unravelled

Community development became a significant tool of social policy in the UK in the late 1960s. It did not suddenly appear, but gradually emerged as an adaptation of the extensive use of the concept in Britain's former colonies, and from the urban programmes of American administrations in the 1950s and 1960s. It had also been pioneered by a number of councils of social service, most notably in London, as a method of helping residents settle in the new towns and housing estates erected in the years after 1945. It had been used, too, in a number of rural areas, including the Scottish Highlands.

Three reports and three government initiatives gave community development a major boost in the last years of the 1960s. These 'establishment' endorsements of community development were themselves energised by the 'street events' of those years and in particular by the thirst of young students to engage in social service, and to give expression to their desire for social justice.

The three reports
The Gulbenkian-sponsored *Younghusband* report of 1968 provided the first reader-friendly account of the purpose, roles and tasks of community developers, and outlined proposals for the incorporation of training for community development in higher education.

The *Seebohm* report, also in 1968, led the way for the creation of unified social services departments, and spelt out the role of the community-oriented social work team. The subsequent creation and expansion of these departments throughout the 1970s provided jobs for community developers and fuelled the expansion of the occupation.

The *Skeffington* report of 1969 drew attention to the need for participation in planning, and in related areas such as housing management. It responded sympathetically to the growing criticism of paternalistic and remote decision-making within local government.

The three government initiatives
These three developments each started, or came to fruition, in 1968, and gave considerable impetus to the growth of community development:

The *Urban Aid* programme provided extensive support for community and voluntary projects, which proved to be major employers of community developers.

The Home Office launched its *Community Development Projects (CDPs)* programme. This comprised teams of both community developers and researchers working together. The CDPs became known less for their grassroots work than for their extensive publications programme which examined the impact of government and business decisions (or the lack of them) on urban areas.

The Department of Education announced the setting up of the *Young Volunteer Force Foundation (YVFF)*. Building on the work of Task Force in London, it was partly conceived as Harold Wilson's Peace Corps initiative, designed to put the energy and caring of young people to work for the needs of the less fortunate, particularly the elderly. It quickly became a mainstream community development agency, running projects in many parts of the UK, mostly in partnership with local authorities. YVFF changed its name to the Community Projects Foundation in 1977, and to the Community Development Foundation in 1989.

It would be foolish to ignore the effect of other events at the end of the 1960s and in the early 1970s which also helped in the establishment of community development. Four in particular should be mentioned: the creation of community relations committees; the transformation of youth work into youth and community work; the re-invigoration of the British settlement movement; and the burgeoning of community arts projects. To these influences might be added the publication in 1973 of the report of the Boyle committee, whose deliberations had been sponsored by the Gulbenkian Foundation. The Boyle report further legitimised community development, but its more lasting effect was to quicken its absorption into the work of other occupations. This was especially to be seen in many church denominations, and in architecture, planning, and housing.

By the early 1980s, community development had also grown in the leisure and recreation departments of local authorities, and had been given a substantial boost by the community programmes of the Manpower Services Commission (MSC). A national survey in 1983 found there were over 5,000 community developers, as well as a large number of other people in related occupations, such as those in councils of voluntary service, community relations officers, welfare rights workers, community artists, adventure playground workers and intermediate treatment staff (Francis et al., 1983).

Decline and uncertainty

Chapter 1 of my 1983 review of community development, *The Making of Community Work*, sought to explain the incoherence within the occupation of community development. Staff were split along employment lines: there were those in national *programmes* such as CDP and CDF; those in local authority *departments*; and those in *projects*, largely in the voluntary sector through the Urban Programme and MSC funding. Incoherence was also created by a number of other factors: the diversity of policy issues in which workers were involved; the absence of local and national strategies for community development; and the uncertain nature of the relationships with host professions such as social work and adult education. In addition, no career structures or patterns emerged. The turnover of community development staff, the absence of a union or association that embraced most staff, and the absence of a common setting or employer accentuated incoherence and fragmentation, as did a lack of consensus about methods and values.

The centrifugal forces acting on community development continued in different ways in the 1980s; a good many posts were lost as various MSC programmes were changed or disappeared, while expenditure cuts led many local authorities and voluntary agencies to dispense with their community workers. Training courses in higher education for community development had all but vanished by the start of the 1990s. The ending of the Urban Programme in England in the early 1990s seriously curtailed the ability of voluntary agencies and local authorities to run community development projects.

Finally, we can note that there were few centripetal forces in community development acting as a holding point at the centre to counterbalance the forces that made for fragmentation. The various associations and federations of community workers in the 1970s and 1980s had neither the members, resources nor credibility to hold the occupation together in even the loosest form of association. Neither the CDPs nor CDF provided a point of coherence for community development; they were seen as remote and unapproachable by most workers based in local authorities and the voluntary sector. Flagship bodies like the National Institute for Social Work and the Community Education Centre rarely attracted community workers outside their own professions. It could be said that for much of the 1970s the Gulbenkian Foundation provided a national point of stability and reference, first through the impact of the Younghusband and Boyle reports, and then through its energetic funding of community development, including race relations, community arts, inner-city partnership schemes and community enterprise. But by 1983, Gulbenkian was moving away from mainstream community development, partly in order to help the voluntary sector cope better with the changes in funding and culture that the Thatcher administration was forcing on it. Community development *as an occupation* thus further unravelled in the 1980s, even though many of its methods and goals *as an intervention* were being absorbed by others.

Community development and the neglect of social process

By the beginning of the 1980s, community development had been firmly lodged in an oppositional or campaign mode: its goals were seen largely as helping local people to oppose the plans of public authorities and/or to win resources from them to improve neighbourhood life. Its emphasis on gaining resources made it predominantly purposive, and task-centred. In addition, the influence of social work and education led community development to an emphasis on change in individuals, rather than change in systems or structures. The twin focus on task and on individual change meant there was a vacuum at the heart of community development because, paradoxically, it did not focus sufficiently on community, or on the notion of its development. In other words, community development managed largely to ignore *social processes* related to the functioning of the community as a system: the quality of relations between people, how decisions are made, conflicts aired, problems solved, people supported and cared for, values and standards defined, control and regulation enforced, and wisdom and traditions passed on.

This matter is looked at in more detail in section 3, but we might note here that the trend in community development in the 1980s was to become *functional*. The decline in oppositional work came about largely as a result of Conservative policies: local authorities were stripped of their powers and funding, and they became part of the victims in society, the institutional dispossessed. Second, local people were in crisis: they needed urgent solutions to pressing problems, particularly unemployment. On top of this, some politicians and civil servants saw community development as a way of stimulating self-help to replace lost services and of managing major problems in society such as rising crime and, of course, unemployment. Community workers became involved in job-creation and job-training schemes. People were excited by community enterprise or local economic development. Functional community development was also involved in housing management, community care delivery and crime prevention. Wherever there was a problem (how do we deliver AIDS prevention programmes to hard-to-reach groups?), community development was tried as a method of service delivery, sometimes with success, sometimes not.

This trend towards problem-solving community projects was reinforced by the increased involvement of the private sector in community programmes. But business was concerned with immediate returns on its investment; it was mostly uninterested in long-term community development. It, too, stressed outcome and product, as well as measurable, concrete achievements. It was profoundly sceptical about what it saw as the mystical language of process and capacity building, unless of course one meant the capacity of individuals.

The combined effect of these and other influences in the 1980s was further to undermine community development's interest and expertise in social process, making it concentrate even more on outcome and product, and pushing it further away from its primary concern with building the capacity of communities. There was, in the language of social work, little interest in system maintenance – in the quality of relationships, networks and interactions between people, and the repair of the social fabric of localities. This is examined further in section 3.

2 Cooperation Through the Data Glass

This section begins with a brief review of CDF's fieldwork projects. The basic facts and figures on the Foundation's field projects are provided, not simply as a record of work over some 25 years, but also as essential background to some of the discussion in the following sections. More importantly, the information on CDF's projects should be seen as a database on *community interaction* in deprived urban areas. I will then link this data to a number of research projects carried out by CDF staff and colleagues in other parts of Europe. This will enable the reader to look at what lies behind the data; namely a commentary on the extent of the contribution local people make to each other's lives, and thus to the quality of the society in which we live.

Between 1968 and 1994, CDF ran 66 projects, mostly in partnership with local and other public authorities. Of these, 19 per cent were in Wales, and 11 per cent in Scotland (there were none in northern Ireland). Of the 42 projects in England, two-thirds were in the north and the midlands (and divided more or less equally between these two areas). A further third were in the south-east and south-west, though only one project was ever based in London. CDF projects were largely in urban areas, often in the inner cities, peripheral housing estates, and in small industrial and mining towns experiencing, or on the edge of, economic decline. Only three projects were in rural areas, though a handful were sited in small rural or sea-side towns and worked in the hinterland. Some of CDF's experience, as well as that of other agencies, in rural areas has been published by Francis and Henderson (1992, 1993, 1994).

Table 1 presents an analysis of the types of projects within the Foundation between 1968 and 1992. It cannot provide a clear-cut picture, as some of the categories will necessarily overlap; for example, much of the employment training work was with young people. Another difficulty is that most of the general community development projects would have included work on housing and employment issues. Indeed, housing or planning were the sole or main focus of almost a third of CDF projects.

It is difficult to convey concisely the nature of work in CDF's projects from 1968 to the present day, and Table 1 gives only a crude overview. Further data on fieldwork are given in my more extended study of CDF (Thomas, 1995).

Table 1 Types of community project in CDF, 1968-1992

Year	H.+TA	Vol SS	YW	GCW	Health	Employ.	Other	Total
68–73	3	9	7	7	1	0	0	27
74–79	3	0	1	3	0	3	1	11
80–85	3	0	1	5	1	6	0	16
86–92	0	0	1	4	1	5	1	12
Total	9	9	10	19	3	14	2	66

Key: H+TA = housing and tenant action *Vol SS* = voluntary social service and/or social education *YW* = youth work, including general youth work, as well as special programmes of education and crime prevention *GCW* = general community work projects, working on a variety of issues with local residents Employ = employment training, job, business and cooperative creation and work around unemployment. The projects have been categorised by the year in which they started. For this reason the Table does not show the number of projects in existence at any one time.

Two main features emerge from Table 1:

First, up until about 1974 CDF was involved in four main areas of work in its projects:

- voluntary social service carried out by young people, usually on behalf of the elderly
- social education; that is, helping schools learn about the communities they worked in
- youth work
- community development.

In all four areas, the Foundation was engaged in new and adventurous work that was to set the pattern for other agencies; for example, there were pioneering attempts to design and implement community studies programmes in schools; youth counselling and detached youth work involving coffee bars; and the development of Arts Laboratories offering young people the chance of theatre workshops, music, dance, painting and motor-cycle repairs. Indeed, long before employee volunteering became fashionable in the late 1980s, CDF in 1971 developed a scheme called Voluntary Social Service in Industry that recruited apprentices and other staff to do voluntary work in their communities.

Second, general community projects accounted for about a third of all projects throughout most of the period. However, there was a trend for these to become more focused on particular issues, as the needs of funders changed. For example, economic issues became more important in the second half of the 1980s as the Urban Programme shifted from social to economic objectives.

How to use these data on CDF's projects

The themes I want to highlight here are not those to do with the success or failure of CDF's projects, or of those concerning the contribution of its community workers as professional enablers. Some of this is dealt with in the next section. The key to opening up the data just presented is this: some 60 field projects found that in each of their localities there were people prepared to work together, without financial reward, to improve things for themselves and their neighbours. The trick is for the reader to see this capacity for interaction (and largely for *cooperative* inter-action) for the wonder that it is, and to view it as a national asset that can be preserved, extended or damaged by the way that policy-makers regard and treat it. We cannot dismiss this capacity for interaction as a rare or isolated phenomenon, because we can deduce from CDF's work that its staff found this capacity in different parts of the country, and over a 25-year period. It was there in a range of urban areas, mostly in deprived communities, and in some rural ones as well. The capacity for interaction was found in a number of policy areas – housing, play, economic development, the environment, community care and so on, indicating that there were virtually no problems that people were not prepared to work on at the local level. And CDF staff found that no issue was too big or too small for people to deal with themselves: the Canterbury People's Group made a successful Estate Action bid for £14.5 million; the Asian and white communities in Sparth-bottoms, Rochdale, worked together to build a community centre that met the cultural and religious needs of both communities. And in Wrexham, a number of local groups came together to establish safe play areas on disused land, to purchase land for outdoor recreation, and to run junior youth clubs and summer play schemes.

In summary, people's capacity for working together was not tied to a particular issue or urban type, or to a particular period in our history, or to a particular political climate or administration. This capacity was present even in periods such as the 1980s when so many influences worked against cooperative effort at local level. These influences included fear of crime, the struggle to survive at a daily level, the prevailing ideologies of self-interest and greed, and the assertion by government of a nation composed only of individuals and families, but not a society, and one in which private enterprise, not public endeavour, was lauded.

Of course, it has to be said now that it is not simply CDF's database of project work that opens our eyes to the evidence of local interaction, but also that of a wide range of other community projects sponsored by other agencies (and by government through the Urban Programme).

Two further points by way of introduction. First, the capacity for working together is not dependent on the presence of altruistic individuals or charismatic leaders. Second, the capacity to cooperate, even in the most deprived communi-ties, is *substantial*; what CDF's experience reveals is that people's working together in their neighbourhoods makes a significant social and economic contribution to the public good. By way of example, we can now turn to examine the scale of local interaction in just one CDF project.

Wrexham Maelor: a case in point

One of the most impressive accounts of local interaction is John Bell's evaluation of CDF's Wrexham Maelor project (1992); it is one of the rare evaluations of community development that uses quantification to assess the outcomes of the work. Some of these techniques are reapplied in the evaluation of the Ogwr project (CDF, 1994), and the Foundation is planning to produce a handbook to make them available for wider use.

The Wrexham Maelor project ran in an urban part of North Wales from 1984 to 1990, supported by the district and county councils. It had a multi-disciplinary staff of ten, some on secondment from the local authorities. The project's aim was to support community life, especially with a view to alleviating the social and economic consequences of unemployment. Its work revolved around helping local people to start up community groups, and then develop their activities. Over the six-year period, 132 community groups were helped by the project, 39 of them intensively. Intensive work comprised helping a group to start up, to develop, to work effectively and to overcome problems and crises. Less intensive work consisted of providing facilities (such as photocopying, a place to meet), contacts and information. The main areas of work of the 39 groups were housing and environment, young people's concerns, education, unemployment, welfare rights advice, arts and crafts, health, play facilities and women's issues. Other groups included elderly people, sports, churches, scouts, community associations, skills training and community newspapers.

Bell went on to look at the numbers of people involved in 32 groups over a five-year period: 278 people were intensively involved, 591 regularly involved as volunteers or members, and some 16,000 people received services such as welfare advice, social events, community newspapers, and play schemes. Working face-to-face with community groups was only the tip of the iceberg; project staff spent much time supporting individuals in the development of their roles and tasks in groups, as well as supporting the social and informal networks upon whose existence and vitality lay much of the success of community groups. Additionally, considerable effort was put into working with local authority staff and members.

Bell's report of the Wrexham project shows how local activity can be stimulated and nurtured through effective community development. The report indicates that:

'The roots of local activity do not lie in professional voluntary organisations – they lie in the smaller but far more numerous kinds of group that arise directly from local community life ... (the Wrexham experience) ... is a vital demonstration both of the universal potential for more independent local activity and of the fact that without specific stimulus much of this potential, especially in areas where people are faced with many social and economic disadvantages, may never be fully realised.'

The extent and role of the community sector

A great deal more information on the extent of local interaction and activity has been provided by CDF's research staff, working with a number of colleagues in six other European countries. The research team studied the extent of local community action in seven urban localities of above-average social and economic disadvantage. The researchers also looked at the role of local groups and organisations, as well as individual actions, informal networks and short-life groups – 'everything which people do beyond their personal and household life to maintain and improve local life …' The researchers found that 'local community action plays a fundamental role in the way people look after themselves and each other, the way they try to improve and manage their surroundings, and the way they try to influence the authorities' (Chanan, 1992). The researchers discovered, in these deprived urban neighbourhoods, on average three groups per 1,000 population, most of which were autonomous residents' organisations. The groups were part of wider informal networks and individual actions designed to help people, and to improve neighbourhood life. The main functions of the groups were:

- organising mutual aid amongst people with a particular need
- providing social and recreational activities
- organising or campaigning for improvements to the locality
- liaising with authorities and articulating needs and problems
- providing information and advice on particular problems
- improving employment opportunities
- providing local communications such as a community newspaper or radio.

Thus the local community sector provides in aggregate a considerable range of services; the study concludes that it is 'relied on in unseen ways to enable society to function, but it is often neglected or treated remotely and insufficiently in public policy'. Whilst community action is a permanent factor in local life, it is also likely to be vulnerable and underdeveloped, especially in deprived communities. It will probably be insecurely and under-resourced, and given little status by policy-makers. Indeed, many policy-makers interviewed as part of the study were largely unaware of the extent and importance of the community sector and the services it delivered. Most were unable to conceive of the web of activity in localities as a sector.

It is, of course, people who drive the sector, and it is helpful to know what predisposes people to become active in their locality. A special survey was carried out in some 1750 households in the seven European urban localities (Bell, 1993). It found that 14 per cent of the community in deprived urban areas were highly or moderately active in local groups and activities. A major finding was that there was no typical sort of person who gets involved in local group activity; altruists were atypical, and self-help was a more powerful motivation for working with others to get things done. Bell identified a 'virtuous circle': the more policy-makers recognise and support local group activity, the more these groups will flourish and attract and motivate individuals, who will in turn be more likely to start or join in local activities that help others.

Both CDF's project experience and its research confirm the importance of helping policy-makers to appreciate the existence and role of the local community sector. This entails recognising that local independent activity has a long-term effect on the inner strength and functioning of a community. It can be supported by treating it as an equal, not junior partner, in service delivery or regeneration, and by ensuring that local groups have some basic resources at their disposal: a place to meet, access to a telephone and office equipment, some seed money, opportunities for training, and good information from and about other partners such as the local authority and businesses.

Community projects supply local neighbourhoods with another resource to help in their activities; community workers strengthen the abilities of core activists and help them to bring more people into participation. Such workers are conduits to experiences, information, funds and other resources that lie outside the locality. More importantly, they can help residents acquire the self-confidence and knowledge *to widen the agenda of local community action*. Much of the concern of spontaneous action in deprived communities is with self-help and mutual aid; CDF's experience shows that an important role of the professional community worker is to help people extend their concerns beyond mutual aid to:

- campaigning or negotiating for resources and improvements
- working on issues they previously thought were outside their ability to influence at the local level; for instance employment or environmental matters
- striking up relationships with people perceived to be 'on another planet', for instance local business people or professionals such as planners or architects who might help with the work of a group
- cooperating with groups in other localities to deal with an issue on a wider geographical basis.

People will almost always cooperate with each other, but community development can substantially *amplify* what they can do, particularly in:

- getting new groups started amongst people who have little or no experience of such involvement
- enabling groups to raise their level of organisation, visibility and credibility with authorities

- enabling them to network more effectively
- helping them bring more people into membership or participation in activities.

Whilst working all the time amongst community groups, neither CDF's field projects, nor community development as a whole, conceived of their collective existence as a sector, and thereby failed to convey to the general public and policy-makers a consciousness of the nature of the beast they were working with. The recently established Community Sector Coalition is now seeking to achieve greater policy recognition of the community sector, *as the major part of the voluntary sector,* but having different concerns from those of professional voluntary organisations, which have wrongly been assumed to represent the whole of the voluntary sector. It is only by conceiving it as a sector that relatively objective indicators and targets can be laid down about its condition in a whole locality, as distinct from the objectives of individual groups, thereby providing proper techniques for a locality-wide strategy of development.

Chanan's justification for describing the activity found in neighbourhoods as a *sector* was not simply the numbers, variety and vitality of autonomous community groups, but also the presence of a range of informal networks that underpinned the effectiveness of the groups, as well as the existence of a number of (mainly informal) umbrella organisations in neighbourhoods. One of the major factors which prevented people from becoming involved in groups was lack of awareness that they existed. Chanan's research showed that very few people knew anything like the full range of community groups in their neighbourhood. Information about community activities is not to be seen simply as a matter of community newspapers, radio, leaflets and fly-posters; more importantly, it depends on effective personal interaction between people in a locality. In a sense, the effectiveness of action within the community sector is largely dependent on the extent and quality of informal community interaction, and it is to this matter that we now turn.

3 The Lost Meaning of Community Development

Many of CDF's projects were in areas where almost the entire population, not just individuals or sub-groups, were experiencing the effects of some form of economic or material deprivation. This was sometimes, as in Clwyd or Dundee, the result of the closure of factories that had been the major employers in an area. Often, too, projects were in areas where housing conditions were poor, and where the lives of residents were further blighted by crime and drug abuse. Sometimes CDF projects operated in areas where there had been no single dramatic event, such as a factory closure, which affected the population, but where there had been a general run-down of employment opportunities and housing conditions, and an erosion of facilities such as shops, pubs, cafes and transport. In addition, people's capacity to cope with stress-causing problems was often weakened by fractured neighbour relationships.

In all these different situations, CDF projects were concerned with the effects of *collective stress*; that is, the whole, or a large part of a community, was suffering. The stress was collective either because large numbers of people were affected by, say, unemployment, and/or because the effects of a problem such as drug abuse or racial violence contaminated the whole fabric of a community's life. The problem of collective stress has more usually been associated with communities that have been affected by a disaster (such as Aberfan and Lockerbie) or by the abduction and murder of children, or by government decisions to locate motorways, noxious industries or prisons in or near them. Those who have written about collective stress as a result of natural disasters, for example, Barton (1969), have tended to describe it in terms of internal or external crises, conflicts and demands which tax or exceed the community's resources to deal with them, and prevent community members from enjoying the conditions of life which they expect from each other or from service-providers.

CDF's experience has helped illuminate the problems of collective stress in a wider range of situations, as well as some of the methods that can be used to remove or ameliorate it. Many CDF projects were, in effect, agencies whose role was to help whole communities develop better ways of coping with persistent and wide-scale stress. By coping, I mean *the capacity of a community to make reasoned decisions about what resources to mobilise in order to make a positive response to various forms of collective stress.* Coping here implies achieving a degree of management and control over stress-causing problems.

Barton's work on natural disasters has shown that a community's ability to cope in a situation of collective stress is determined by:

- the willingness of people to talk with each other
- their knowledge of the extent of there being a common problem
- a sympathetic identification with each other
- the existence of norms about mutual help.

In short, a community's response to crisis will depend greatly on the extent and vitality of, first, the *social resources* within it – resources such as trust, empathy, cooperation, mutuality, caring, a sense of justice, leadership, self-image and identity, and, second, its *social processes* of communication, interaction, exchange and problem-solving.

Barton's work on coping with disasters should have been a salient clue to community workers in the early 1970s that fostering community interaction was as important a long-term goal as organising people into community action groups was in the short term. Clues from other disciplines about development processes were also largely ignored, including those from social anthropology; a point to which I will return below.

The meaning of community development

Community development strengthens the social resources and processes in a community, by developing those *contacts, relationships, networks, agreements and activities* outside the household, that residents themselves identify will make their locality a better place to live and work in. In some circumstances, the successful initiation of this process will require the help of an enabler (mostly called a community worker in the UK, and mostly intervening from 'outside' as a professional). It will always require some participation by local government, the professional voluntary sector and business.

By this definition, there has never been a national programme of community development in the UK. What we have seen is the burgeoning of community workers and community projects given the time (usually three years) sufficient only to help local people improve resources in their locality, with little or no attention to relationships, networks, activities and agreements – that is to the extent and quality of social interaction and consensus between people outside the immediate household. In brief, community development became reduced to short-term community projects focussed largely on improving resources. Long-term capacity building became subsumed to short-term problem fixing. Equally, the need to create action groups to solve particular problems often led to the overlooking of pre-existing networks and groups that were more involved with mutual aid, or perhaps with social and recreational activities. Of course, the resource-centred approach to community development was encouraged because improving locality resources was what residents themselves were most often concerned about.

Furthermore, there has been little recognition of the role and value of community development *in its own right*, rather policy-makers have tried to use it as a universal social spanner, to fix-'n'-mend problems that they themselves have often created. Within CDF's own experience, for example, government has tried community development to prevent crime, regenerate local economies, cut the costs of custodial care, and promote health education. Even the government's own so-called national programme of community development projects set up in 1968 was established to deal with family breakdown and rising juvenile delinquency. This attitude, incidentally, implies that 'community' is something only needed when other things go wrong – not a good in itself. Community development agencies have been impelled to collude with this fix-'n'-mend approach in order to attract government and private sector funding; in order to help agencies stay in business, an incomplete form of community development has been presented as a panacea for a range of social and economic problems. As a result, scepticism about community development has increased, since it would have been impossible for community development adequately to fulfil all the claims of its proponents or the dreams of policy-makers to whom it was being sold for a (quick and cheap) solution to their difficulties.

The crisis of poverty: leadership

The concern of community workers with poverty, and particularly with achieving material gains such as improved housing or better play facilities, has also led to a emphasis on leadership. Effective leaders were needed to form and galvanise residents groups to deal with improving neighbourhood resources. This focus on leadership was reinforced by the interest in business in empowerment, and the cultivation of community entrepreneurs. The idea of the empowerment of individuals was taken up by government who talked enthusiastically of the 'active citizen'. A feature of the 1980s that reflected the concern with individual leadership was the proliferation by business, often in partnership with the voluntary sector, of award schemes and prizes to reward individuals for their work in their communities. The concern with capacity building was too narrowly seen as the capacity of individuals, rather than that of building the capacity of communities through strengthening social resources and processes; in many cases, this has in the long term been as self-defeating as an army strengthening the fighting prowess of individual soldiers without giving them the means to communicate with each other, and understand their respective roles within a corporate battle plan. This emphasis on the individual-in-the-community by business and government was all the more puzzling because of the over riding concern with corporate strategies and team-playing to be found in business; there was, in a sense, a failure to transfer the learning about corporate culture to the way that communities could be developed to achieve their particular goals to be better places to live and work in.

The crisis of belonging: membership

The development of leadership is important but it has overshadowed the equally significant part of membership – that is, how people experience being in contact and relations with each other outside the household, their sense of individual and common identity, and the ways in which they see themselves contributing, or not, to the area in which they live.

The concept of membership is better than that of leadership as a way in to understanding the meaning that a particular locality has for the people who live in it. When residents say they live in a 'good' community they usually mean that their locality gives them a chance to go smoothly about the daily business of living and earning a living; that it provides a decent environment to bring up children, and to care for those in need; and that it allows people the chance to make something of their lives and themselves, to meet their aspirations. They also mean that it is easy to meet people, it has a good atmosphere, a sense of reciprocity, and there are others they can call upon in time of trouble. More significantly, a community that is functioning well is one whose residents can take up new opportunities, and also one in which residents are able to confront, and not be overwhelmed by, challenges, difficulties and problems. In other words, in functioning communities residents have a sense that they can influence the events that will affect their lives, they are able to set goals for collective neighbourhood life, and they are able to work together to achieve those goals. On the other hand, in communities that are not working well, residents will experience feelings of hopelessness, dependence on others to do things, and often passivity and frustration that can erupt into violence.

In communities that hold positive meaning for those who live there, there is opportunity for independent thought and action, a capacity for people to work together to achieve goals held in common, whether it be the setting up of a baby-sitting system, running a food cooperative, putting on a summer play scheme, cleaning up the environment, or resisting plans for a motorway or chemical recycling plant. Reviewing anthropological experience, Goodenough has suggested that the culture of a community that gives it positive meaning for residents consists of 'standards for deciding what is, standards for deciding what can be, standards for deciding how one feels about it, standards for deciding what to do about it, and standards for deciding how to go about it' (1963, pp. 258–259).

In other words, these 'standards' are simply *understandings or agreements* about how people living together in a locality manage their everyday affairs outside the household. It is the presence or absence of these agreements (or, more significantly, of the means to reach these agreements) that will determine the health or effective functioning of localities. Here again we find a further failure on the part of those concerned with the state of British communities to transfer to communities knowledge from other disciplines and areas of social life. There is widespread agreement about the 'contractual' nature of other social units in our lives; we understand that relationships in, say, the family, work place, school, hospital or sports club, depend largely on their members overtly or tacitly having agreements about behaviour, rights and responsibilities; but we have been largely unable to see that part of the wellbeing of people living together in localities also depends on similar, sometimes unspoken, 'contracts' about living together.

Schoenberg's research in America (1980) confirms the basic ingredients of a healthy (or what she calls a viable) community along the lines indicated by Goodenough, and earlier by Barton in communities affected by natural disasters. Schoenberg's extensive research in a range of communities shows that viable communities tend to have:

- ways in which residents can exchange information between themselves
- opportunities to discuss differences and conflicts
- ways of agreeing upon shared standards of public behaviour; for example, the behaviour of children on the streets, the disposal of rubbish, the upkeep of public parts of a locality
- ways to identify communal problems and their possible solutions
- opportunities to set collective goals to tackle those problems
- access to skills and resources needed to achieve those goals successfully, including the means to identify leaders and knowledge-holders within their own ranks, and access to resource-holders outside.

The capacity to manage daily life outside the household is thus clearly dependent on the extent to which people recognise each other as neighbours; have contact with each other in a way that facilitates sharing information; participate in a range of formal and informal community activities; and come to agreements about living together.

In short, the coping community is an interactive and participatory one, though how many people will be participatory in events and groups will vary with factors like class, age, and whether or not they are employed, or have children. It will also be affected by matters such as lack of mobility, due to poor transport, fear of sexual or racial harassment, or being tied by care responsibilities (see Chanan, 1992). It is the strength and variety of this interaction that allows residents to have a sense of control over their well-being, to come to agreements ('standards') for living together, and to pool their various resources, time and energies in problem-solving activities.

A ladder of community interaction

The fundamental concern at the heart of community development with social resources and processes can be made more concrete, in a way that is suggestive of what other professionals might contribute to the development of viable communities. Viable or coping communities will:

- exist or be designed in a way that brings residents together rather than keeps them apart from one another
- have facilities that promote social contact, such as pubs, churches, shops, cafés, community centres and so on
- have daily routines that promote interaction between people; for example walking children to school rather than taking them by car
- have a variety of 'live' social and recreational networks, as well as those based on mutual aid
- have active organisations of a variety of kinds and purposes that bring people together and which define and represent their ideas and concerns
- allow residents to take on public roles outside the household that are satisfying to themselves and of service to others.

This can be shown as a ladder of community interaction:

11.	Owning and managing local facilities
10.	Working with policy-makers
9.	Co-operation with other community groups
8.	Joining community groups
7.	Participating in community activities
6.	Informal mutual aid
5.	Involvement in informal networks
4.	Social contacts; such as at the pub, church or community centre
3.	Routine contacts; such as picking the children up from school every day
2.	Casual contacts; for example whilst shopping or waiting for the bus
1.	Mutual recognition

At the base of the ladder are the routine, trivial and taken-for-granted aspects of community interaction, yet they are the foundation on which all else rests. The existence and vitality of the more formal organisation of community life above the dotted line will depend in part on the working of the more casual networks below. These contacts below the dotted line make up the round of daily life outside the household, and their importance is not to be underestimated if we want to create communities that work. Summarising his own and others' work, Peter Willmott writes that these so-called routine and trivial contacts help residents to locate themselves in the wider structure of the community, helping to make sense of their lives in what might otherwise be a complex and anonymous world (1989). Writing of the importance of casual and informal interaction, Jane Jacobs (1972, p. 67) observes:

> 'Most of it is ostensibly trivial, but the sum is not trivial at all. The sum of such casual, public contact at local level – most of it fortuitous, most of it associated with errands – is a feeling for the public identity of people, a web of public respect and trust, and a resource in time of personal or neighbourhood need.'

The absence or infrequency of interactions between residents produces what may be called the *nominal* community – one in which households live together but where residents have few, if any, interactions with each other. This may be an effective community for some people, particularly for those who do not need their neighbours to help them with problems or tasks. These, if you like, are the 'privileged': they have a choice about how far their social life is constituted around the family, the neighbourhood or groups and people outside in a wider geographical area. (Here I am indebted to Saunders (1986)). If they have problems, they can often choose how to solve them (with a relative? neighbour? someone at the golf club?) or have the resources to buy in expert advice. The 'underprivileged' are those who have no choice in how their social life is constituted, and have to face difficulties with a limited or absent set of relations built around local neighbours, with little access to solutions to problems outside their neighbourhood or through commercial services. (It is worth noting that the divide between privileged and under-privileged may occur within a family: one spouse with job, car and membership of recreational clubs may not know of the extent of the isolation of the other spouse working at home as child carer, or unemployed.)

Thus part of the purpose of community development is to help the 'under-privileged' develop a social life around local neighbour relations, and to use this local framework to solve individual and collective problems. Besides poverty and material deprivation, communities are underprivileged when their inhabitants are unable to communicate with each other in order to form agreements about both the daily tasks of living together, and how to deal with particular problems that crop up in the life of any locality.

Most community projects in the UK operated at rung 7 (such as organising a community festival) or 8 (for example, forming a tenants' association) of the ladder of community interaction. This type of organising was needed and responded to people's urgent material needs. It was often successful in winning much-needed resources, or providing opportunities for job training or self-employment. But capacity building it wasn't, because it was mostly detached from the lower rungs of the ladder. The responsibility for this lies only partly with community workers; it mainly belongs with their employers and policy-makers who gave them so little in terms of resources, time and support, and whose vision was so limited that they wished to accomplish only short-term tasks, material outcomes, and change in individuals rather than in the social fabric of communities themselves.

4   Community Projects: Tasks, Outcomes and Evaluation

The previous section suggested that the setting up of community projects was a limited expression of the meaning and potential of community development. Nevertheless, such projects have been a substantial part, largely through the Urban Programme, of government and voluntary initiatives in coping with urban decline and deprivation. The range of community projects within CDF was indicated in section 2.

The tasks of the workers in most community projects were to:

* help local people form groups to take action to improve neighbourhood life on those issues of most concern to them. This usually involved helping groups bring new resources into the area.
* provide the advice and support necessary for the groups to achieve their goals. This had four elements:

  (a)   how to access resources, including a place to meet, telephone, photocopier, typewriters and the like, that a group needed to carry out its work
  (b)   advice and information on the particular issue a group was working on, such as housing legislation
  (c)   advice on tactics and strategy in matters like negotiating with the council
  (d)   advice on maintaining the effectiveness of the group; that is, helping it to grow in confidence, to learn how to overcome setbacks, as well as difficulties such as rivalry and quarrels, and to acquire the skills needed for a committee to operate efficiently and democratically.

* help groups develop effective relationships with others in the area, and also with resource holders in the public and private sectors. Relationships with resource holders sometimes involved conflict as well as partnership, particularly in the period from 1968 to 1980.
* enable groups to develop over time to become more self-sufficient and autonomous.

The difficulties in evaluating outcomes in this kind of work have been well documented, not least in an early CDF publication, which still remains a standard text on the subject (Key et al., 1976). Evaluation in community development has always been bedevilled by the difficulties facing workers in recording, monitoring and describing what it is they have been doing. There has always been a reluctance, too, to give the impression of claiming credit that is due to local people themselves. In addition, funders have been slow to commit the resources necessary for proper evaluation. Community development in local authority departments, especially social services, was usually viewed as secondary to a department's 'main work', and was not accorded the respect and resources needed for evaluation.

The general failure to evaluate community projects (mirrored in CDF's own patchy attempts at evaluation) was chiefly the result of a lack of will and resources, not of the difficulties of methodology. My experience at CDF showed me that I was wrong ten years ago to describe the methodological problems as 'formidable' (Thomas, 1983), except perhaps in relation to evaluating changes in local people's knowledge and self-confidence (see below). Most community projects were staffed by single workers or small teams, and such was the pressure of work on them that they had little time and energy to monitor and evaluate. Moreover, many had not been trained to do so.

Of course, practitioners have always been cynical and suspicious about evaluation, believing it to be reductionist, and largely an opportunity for academics to make money out of poverty; but, curiously, there has been little academic interest in research in community development. Social scientists have tended to stay clear of the field (see Thomas, 1983, pp 268-271). This general lack of interest in evaluation exacerbated the difficulties that agencies such as CDF experienced in developing more systematic forms of evaluation. There were, too, problems with the credibility of evaluation and those who required it, not least because the results of an evaluation were not necessarily taken into account when decisions were made about whether projects were to continue. Such decisions were more likely to be political than rational. Fisker (1992, p. 12) has confirmed this in his evaluation of the Danish Social Development Programme: the single most important factor in whether or not a project continued was its location; projects located wholly or partly in local authorities were more likely to continue than those in the voluntary sector. And large projects were more likely to continue than smaller ones.

Outcomes in community projects

It is possible to see from CDF's experience that the following are the outcomes that might be expected of community projects. They help to illustrate that it is possible to provide quantitative assessments of the work of community projects.

Development of people's skills, knowledge and confidence

This has been the most difficult area to measure. There have been no systematic 'before and after' assessments of local people who have been helped by community projects, and there would be a good number of theoretical, practical and moral objections to doing so. Such experiments would be anathema to most community workers, whose relations with local people would be disturbed if the latter thought they were being used as guinea-pigs. Many CDF case studies contain comments from local people about their own individual progress. In the Bedworth Heath project, for example, residents remarked:

'We've learnt so much. When I first went to a meeting, I knew nothing about anything ... I didn't even know what a constitution was.'

'When I started going to meetings, I only listened. I didn't talk or participate but I found that slowly I was getting the answers to the questions that I had.'

'The most important thing the project has done to this estate is education.'

'Before their resources came here, there wasn't any of us that are now involved that had the knowledge.'

In short, people have learnt to run meetings and organise events, and to develop practical skills such as minute-taking, book-keeping, writing letters and so on. There has been learning, too, about local authority structures and decision-making, as well as about policy areas such as housing, play or environmental health. In addition, some projects ran specialist training courses for local people on subjects like playgroup leadership, welfare rights advice and the development of community businesses. This building of local capacity for independent and thoughtful action has been an achievement in CDF projects and more generally throughout community work. But it is quite remarkable that there has been no systematic (and published) account of local people's perceptions of community projects and their staff. This is a considerable paradox, that an occupation so attached to giving a voice to local people has failed in helping them speak about the work of the occupation itself.

The formation of community groups
There are no data available which indicates the total numbers of groups helped by CDF projects to start up and/or become more effective in their activities. However, the evaluation of the Wrexham project (see section 2) gives an indication of the level of activity to be associated with a well-resourced community project (there were seven field workers in that project). Similarly, CDF's Ogwr project worked with 26 groups intensively, providing 50 others with more background support.

Bringing in resources
Most community projects are concerned with helping residents find ways of bringing in new resources and facilities to their neighbourhood. These may range from play schemes, housing refurbishment, credit unions to pedestrian crossings.

Attracting such resources was central to much of the work in CDF's projects. In south Wales, for example, the Ogwr Valleys team helped residents in Bettws, an outlying housing estate, to attract government and private sector support totalling some £600,000 to refurbish a derelict community hall, open a community cafe, purchase an historic chapel, establish a family centre and landscape an overgrown and neglected area of the estate. No attempt was made by CDF, nor by community projects elsewhere, to record the kind and value of resources brought into areas where its teams operated.

Training, jobs and businesses

CDF ran a number of training workshops funded by the MSC to develop work skills amongst unemployed young people. It also ran projects primarily concerned with job creation and placement through community businesses, workspace development and cooperatives. There were 14 projects in all devoted to this area of work. However, there are no data available to indicate the total numbers of jobs, businesses and training places provided. Some projects were independently evaluated however, and show that quantitative data can be successfully generated. For example, the 'Self-Start in Business' scheme, run by the CDF team in Newport and funded by Monsanto UK, generated 677 proposals from young people in Gwent between 1985 and 1988 for business start-ups or expansions. Of these, 381 led to applications to the Newport team for help in development. 131 fully developed business plans were submitted, and of these, 67 grants were made from the Monsanto fund. By 1989, 51 of these new businesses were still trading, providing employment for 156 people, or the equivalent of 134 full-time jobs. The cost per job created was £543 – an extremely competitive figure compared with most other job-creation schemes (see Rumbles, 1990).

Stimulating voluntary activity

By their very nature and intent, community projects stimulate voluntary activity, usually through people's involvement in community groups and events. And projects often stimulate voluntary activity by people who would not normally be volunteers – unemployed people, for example, or those isolated through poverty or disability. Bell has broken new ground in his Wrexham evaluation (1992) by quantifying the number of hours of voluntary effort in groups supported by the Wrexham project. He also uses, though with some qualification, a formula that calculates the relationship between the time put in by the paid community workers and the number of hours of voluntary activity of group members This calculation indicates that each hour of professional input by the Wrexham team produced some 15 hours of voluntary work by local people.

Fundraising

The amount of money (from trusts, government and business) brought into an area by community groups aided by community projects easily lends itself to quantification. However, few data of this kind are available from CDF projects or other community initiatives. Again, we need to look at the efforts of one or two projects as an indicator of what is possible, and what may have been achieved, but not recorded, through community projects. The CDF project in the Ogwr valleys, for example, helped community groups raise over £1,800,000 million in a five-year period.

Income Growth

Many of CDF's projects helped people on state benefits to work out their proper entitlements, and thus to bring more income into the household. These welfare rights campaigns were often focused on a particular estate or neighbourhood, so it would have been possible to quantify the increase in income in an area as a result of a project's work. But whilst a number of CDF annual reports indicate the size of the increase in claims, there is no information on the amount of cash brought in as the result of one project's work, nor for all the projects engaged in promoting the take-up of entitlements.

Of these measures, only the first, the development of people's skills and knowledge, does not lend itself to the production of output data. It is also clear from CDF's experience that there are also other possibilities for quantitative measurement. For example, it would certainly be possible to devise some measures of resources saved. There have been many projects, including some at CDF, set up to reduce crime and its associated costs; others, such as CDF's Dewis project, were established to show how community-based work with young offenders could cut the re-offending rate, as well as save on the substantial costs of custodial care. The 1990 report on Dewis, produced by Clwyd social services, showed that the cost per week per youngster of being on the Dewis programme was £150. This represented considerable savings for the local authority over the costs of prison custody (£291–£361 per week) and over the costs of residential care in an open community home (£400–£900 per week) A similar range of savings was found in CDF's Reading project with young offenders, which was taken on by the social services department in 1986.

The impact on local policy

One of the most significant features of CDF's fieldwork is that, after about 1976, it was mostly goal-centred. That is, the projects, having established the needs and interests of local people and the public authorities, worked to a set of explicit goals, mostly linked to the improvement of the resource base of an area. Attainment of these goals – whether concerned with housing, crime prevention or economic development – was backed by strong management from CDF headquarters. The Foundation was remarkable in the degree of management direction and support it was able to give its field staff from the mid-1970s onwards – in contrast to management in many parts of the voluntary sector, for example, or that in local authority departments, who rarely understood the goals of community development, or the management and personal support needs of the staff of its community projects.

CDF's impact on local policy can be assessed by using three categories developed by Fisker (1992, p. 12) in his evaluation of the Danish government's Social Development Programme which, between 1988 and 1991, gave $55million to local municipalities to:

'... strengthen local initiative ... to promote locally based development work in order to strengthen the local community ... to provide improved opportunities for people for self-expression and participation in the decision-making processes pertaining to their everyday lives.'

Fisker's three criteria for evaluating impact are as follows.

Continuation

Has the project continued after the initial period has finished? We can say that CDF was able to demonstrate the value of its community projects, and to promote their adoption by many of the local authorities within which it worked. A third of CDF projects between 1980 and 1989 were extended by invitation of the local authorities after the first term had expired; and a third of projects (not necessarily the same projects in this third) were absorbed by the local authority or went independent after CDF's withdrawal.

Rub-off

How do experiences from one project spread within a local authority and to other authorities? It is significant that over half of CDF projects from 1968 to the present day were in authorities, or neighbouring authorities, where there had previously been a CDF project. In some cases such as Clwyd, Gwent and Greater Manchester there were four or five projects in the period, each dealing with some new aspect of community well-being. In Clwyd, for example, the first project was started in response to the closure of the Shotton steel works; it was followed by projects on housing, work with young offenders and community libraries. In many locations, CDF projects had what one correspondent called 'a profound impact on local policy-making.' CDF was able to promote an understanding of community development in areas where it had previously not been accepted or understood, including rural areas, small industrial towns and peripheral housing estates. In addition: 'CDF was good at stimulating community-based action and particularly helped some local authorities to become receptive to groups in the community who they might otherwise have regarded as hostile and obstructive.' Most CDF projects succeeded, too, in bringing together a range of local players; they had an integrating value, and thus many were modelling the kind of partnership approach to regeneration that is becoming more significant today.

The rub-off effect of most projects was local, confined to a local authority or region, except for those which produced reports that were published by CDF. A handful received national attention: some because of controversy (Nottingham) and some because the value of their work was seen to have wider applicability (the work with young offenders by the Dewis project, for example, had influence throughout Wales). Rub-off was also facilitated from the mid-1980s onwards by a more effective dissemination programme within CDF, particularly through publications, conferences and seminars.

Learning

Was any new understanding gained by those in local authorities involved in the project? There were three areas of learning; CDF projects:

- helped many local authorities to understand both the value and mechanics of more participative decision-making, and of more accessible local services. Many projects demonstrated the way to better tenant participation and management in housing and environmental decisions; and projects such as Wrexham and Rochdale had a major influence on the policies of the local authority to decentralise town hall functions to neighbourhood level
- played a part in promoting amongst local authorities the ideas of local economic development through community businesses, and other forms of neighbourhood enterprise
- were able to show how to use community projects in policy areas in which they had not previously been seen as relevant. These included intermediate treatment, crime prevention, health issues such as AIDS and stress, library information services, and rural issues.

In all of these areas, CDF showed the value of constructive partnerships between local authorities and community groups. In a real sense, the projects thus helped to rehabilitate the credibility of community development, which had been damaged amongst many authorities by the demise of the government's CDP programme, and by the aggressive stance (much of it justified) of community battles against local authorities in the late 1960s and early 1970s.

From the mid-1980s onwards, the impact on local authorities was strengthened when CDF opened up regional offices to manage its projects and to work directly, and more closely, with authorities in the region. At the same time, CDF's influence was extended through its regional and local conferences directed at the public sector, and through its collaboration with the Association of Metropolitan Authorities in a number of national conferences and publications on community development.

By the mid-1980s, CDF had begun to find 'a third way' in the design and management of community projects. This was to be an alternative to the two primary models of the earlier decade; the first had been the employment of community workers within departments of the local authority, usually one worker attached to, for instance, a social services area team. The second had been the growth of community projects in the voluntary sector, largely through Urban Aid funding. These were usually for three years, with one or two workers, who often had to work with inadequate resources and support. Neither of these two models had dealt effectively with the challenge of incorporating community development within strategic and team goals; as a result the practice of community development had largely been individualistic, and marginal to the work of most employing agencies.

CDF's third way

CDF's most significant step forward in reducing the marginality of community projects was the design of the *large* community team. By 1984, for example, half of CDF's community projects (not including the employment training projects) comprised six or more members, and some had twice this number or more. Larger teams meant increased effectiveness, not simply through having an adequate level of resourcing, but also through creating teams that were purposively multi-disciplinary. Being multi-disciplinary usually meant that more than one local authority department was involved, and this strengthened the independence of the team. The increasing use of secondees from local authority departments, and the strategic use of project management committees with senior local representation, also helped to 'bed-in' a project.

The emergence of the large team was sometimes accompanied by a change in terminology; the community project became the community *Agency*, in an attempt to denote the greater salience of the team within the public sector structure.

Why the community Agency evolved

The notion of the Agency had evolved in response to what CDF called the distance between local (and national) government and the people they purported to serve:

'Departments of government ... remain isolated and distanced from the effects of their action on local people. They are unable to judge the effectiveness of their policies and cannot extend their impact into many sectors of the population. They

are unable to respond flexibly to new ideas, new information or changed circumstances ... there is little or no strategic overview in local authorities to
draw together policies and action as they affect individuals, neighbourhoods and
different local government departments ... major tranches of money for, say inner
cities, are in fact spent without benefit of an operational strategy although
there are frequently broadbrush political strategies. The consumers of the
services from these programmes are not involved in any way' (CDF internal Policy
Paper, 1985)

The reasons for this malaise, reflected the policy paper, were 'high wall depart-
mentalism, the inertia of large bureaucracies and the very ordinary desire on
many individuals' parts to play safe'. The paper also accepted that in the past
community projects had been sidelined by local authority departments, whose officers
and members as principal funders could control the work of the project in ways that
may not have been in the best interests of local communities. Thus the community
Agency was designed to weaken the control of a single local authority department
by bringing in a range of departmental interests.

It was also designed to prevent community projects staff from working in an ad
hoc and random way to their own agendas. The Agency was meant to reflect team
goals, for which it would clearly be accountable to the local community and public
authorities. What also distinguished the Agency from the old-type project was its
staffing: there were experienced community workers, as well as secondees from local
authority departments with a range of other skills at their disposal. This, when taken
with senior local authority representation in the management of the agency, was
to enable staff 'to tackle targets in the local authority at different points in the
hierarchy and across departments'.

Above all, CDF had recognised that the often self-imposed marginality
of community workers, as well as that imposed by departments more
concerned with their 'main work', could only be overcome *if space to act in the
community was negotiated.* This was an important insight into the notion of a community
Agency. Community workers had no statutory expressions of their right to act in
the community, nor were there any common ethics and professional standards
accepted within community development, and more crucially by its funders and
employers, which defined the boundaries of action with and within the community.
Therefore, argued the CDF policy paper:

'space to act has to be negotiated and agreed. The community development
agency is a good structure for this, allowing community workers negotiated space
to act, and holding them accountable for their work ... an agency does not and
must not allow workers to do just what they wish to do. All fieldworkers in CDF
are ... paid intervenors. They are held accountable for their actions by CDF
management. CDF itself is held accountable ... by elected councillors'.

The 1980 Hulbert Home Office review of CDF had described the emerging ideas of the community Agency as:

'a major contribution to the development of community work ... Despite CDF's apparent difficulties in collating and sharing its experience, its field work does demonstrate a pattern of learning. There is a progression in methods of intervention of which the 'agency' is the current pinnacle of achievement.'

But by the mid-1980s events were to conspire to prevent the development of the agency concept. These included the extensive cuts in local authority powers and resources imposed by central government, which undermined the capacity of local authorities to fund the kind of agency being developed at CDF. In addition, changes were also afoot at CDF to reduce its own commitment to fieldwork, and to put more of its own resources into regionalisation and dissemination. The agency concept disappeared, but its importance lay in recognising that the marginality of community projects could be ameliorated by properly structured and managed teams, working to openly agreed work programmes in the space negotiated with local people and the local authority. This, of course, was the space that Jones et. al. had termed *interjacence* (1980). Whilst they had described this as a necessary characteristic of community development, it was CDF that had begun to evolve, through the agency concept, the kind of vehicle that could fully exploit interjacence, and through the large team lessen the marginality experienced by community projects.

CDF's influence at national level

'CDF's failure was not to put community development on the map in a more coherent and explicable and practical way'.

'CDF has failed to explain to the world at large just what community development is, and why it is an important tool of social policy and practice ... but then so have all other community development organisations.'

The charge of failure made by two correspondents to this study may be rather harsh; the failure in communicating to two decades of policy-makers the value of community development lies, first, as much with other community development organisations and other players such as academics and researchers; and, second, with the adverse political climate of the 1970s and the 1980s in which neither Labour nor Conservative administrations placed much value on collective self-help at the local level. Of equal importance in explaining the policy failure at national level was the drive in community development to self-effacement, and its own failure to develop a set of national institutions devoted to community development, or even a coherent national forum, the need for which was first identified in the Boyle report of 1973. I have already described and explained the incoherence within community development (see the Introduction), as well as the absence of 'glue' or bonding to hold the disparate parts of the occupation together. It is these characteristics of community development which have been as important in its failure to influence policy as the work of any particular organisation, such as CDF, and they provide the context for the discussion below about the Foundation.

On the face of it, CDF's status as a quango of the Voluntary Services Unit (VSU) at the Home Office offered the opportunity for access to policy-making about, for example, inner-city issues, where community development was highly relevant. In fact, this status cut little ice in government departments, because the Home Office was not regarded as a significant player in the regeneration policies of the 1980s, which were led, on the whole, by the Department of Trade and Industry (DTI) and the Department of the Environment (DoE). The VSU itself was largely regarded as a funding body, not a policy-making one, and was mainly associated with traditional forms of voluntarism, and not with community development, capacity building and empowerment. Nor was there any other department in central government that 'looked after' community development and could press for its incorporation into the inner city policies of the Thatcher administrations. A further factor that impeded both CDF and community development was the nervous and ambivalent feelings about the 1970s CDP programme that were still evident in government departments well into the late 1980s.

For most of the 1980s, ministers and civil servants were more interested in economic outputs from community initiatives than social ones, and more inclined to work with the private sector than with local authorities. Both these factors worked against CDF and community development in general. CDF's experience was almost wholly about partnerships with local authorities, and it was unable convincingly to translate that experience into the new market ethos that was emerging. Indeed, its own links with the private sector did not materialise until the early 1990s. The very fact that CDF and community development were so inextricably linked with local authorities was itself a blot on the prospectus for community development that was presented to policy-makers in the 1980s.

The Foundation's work in relation to economic regeneration was significant in its own portfolio of fieldwork. There were a number of successful projects in this area, but CDF only partially succeeded in passing on its lessons from this area of work to policy-makers. The main reasons for this were that, first, policy-makers were sceptical about the contribution of community enterprises to macro-regeneration strategies; and, second, even where they were prepared to listen and take advice, they chose to go to specialist agencies (such as CEI and Community Business Scotland) dealing with local economic development, or to private sector consultants, rather than to a generalist agency like CDF whose interest in the field was only partial.

This indeed was an example of a more general difficulty: CDF was an expert in a method of intervention called community development; this method was relevant to a wide range of policy areas (economic development, housing and the environment, social work, health and education and so on) but the Foundation was never able to deploy enough staff who were expert in community development *and* who were seen as experts in particular policy areas. The tendency of policy-makers was to turn to the agencies or academics who were specialists in particular areas, and to ask them about community development, even though their expertise in this field was generally limited.

Even close to its own backyard, CDF failed to make the impact that was commensurate with its experience. The government's concern in the late 1980s with the active citizen provides an example. Civil servants, including those at VSU, were unable to move away, or persuade Ministers to move away, from a traditional view of volunteering, and little ground was made in convincing them of the extent and value of that kind of active citizenship to be found in neighbourhood groups and networks. Policy-makers continued to seek advice from the specialist agencies in (traditional) volunteering, and what efforts were made to stimulate more volunteering (for instance employee volunteering) tended to draw more volunteers from the white, in-work and middle-class background that was characteristic of British volunteering. Neither CDF nor any other agency made much headway in extending the profile of volunteering from the 'the volunteer' to 'those engaged in voluntary action'.

Curiously, CDF had more success in the late 1980s and early 1990s in promoting community development in the private sector. This was largely due to the invaluable work previously done by Business in the Community, which had made the case for corporate involvement in community initiatives. But in addition, many in the private sector were practically and intuitively closer to some of the goals and values of community development than civil servants were, because of the importance many of them attached to the customer/consumer. And by the nature of their jobs in industry and retailing, they had considerable more contact with 'real life' than many civil servants did. The latter were also driven by Ministers to devise grand programmes for regeneration that would attract good publicity for both Ministers and the government as a whole. They were less interested in the development of small-scale, and inevitably low-profile, community projects. Many private sector personnel, on the other hand, disparaged the grand programme and were more interested in grassroots projects empowering real people, and with whom their local and regional staff could develop a meaningful partnership.

Many of these issues can be summed up by saying that there is an in-built capacity in community development (and in many of its agencies, such as CDF) to be marginalised by its own success. There have been periods since the late 1960s when community development has been successful in motivating a large number of occupations that have absorbed and implemented many of its values and methods. This was most clearly seen in the development of community social work, the community business movement, community-based crime prevention schemes, community architecture and planning, community education and, to a lesser extent, community health. As these movements gained and lost ground (an up-to-date account of these trends has been produced by Butcher et al, 1993), they did not naturally turn to agencies in community development such as CDF for leadership and advice; *more often than not, they devised their own structures and institutions.* Likewise, as the business community developed its involvement in communities, it spawned its own lead agencies such as Business in the Community and Action Resource Centre. One of community development's major achievements, and one in which CDF played, and still plays, a substantial part (see Smith, 1992; Blewitt and Garratt, 1993, 1995) is the development of the tenant participation movement, and the incorporation of schemes for tenant participation in housing management. Here again, the percolation of community development ideas (and years of hard work carried out with tenants by community projects) led to the growth of agencies such as the Tenant Participation Advisory Service to carry forward the work started within community development. There are a range of other examples, but these are enough to show that the major objective set out in the Younghusband (1968) and Boyle (1973) reports to influence the policies and practice of other occupations has been substantially achieved. The cost, however, has been that of marginalising community development as an intervention and as a distinctive occupation, a process that was inevitably hastened by the wide-scale cuts in community development posts in the 1980s in local authorities and the voluntary sector.

5 Conclusions: From Despair to Realistic Appraisal

I believe there are four major lessons to be learnt from the experience of community projects in the UK:

First, that local people in even the most difficult of circumstances are prepared to cooperate and work together to improve their lives and the place where they live.

Second, that there is hardly any part of neighbourhood life (housing, employment, play, community care and so on) where this disposition to work together cannot be activated.

Third, that people's efforts can be substantially amplified by access to resources (for instance, a place to meet) and help from professional enablers such as community workers.

Fourth, that the effectiveness of these workers can be enhanced through a large-team approach to community development. The practice of locating community workers in small projects, or within teams of other professionals such as social workers, has hampered their ability to carry out both neighbourhood work and developmental work with public authorities.

It is sometimes very difficult to retain one's optimism about the impact of community development, not least in those periods when a government department announces its latest initiative for urban regeneration, inviting the cooperation of local authorities, and of 'the community.' There will usually be lip-service paid to the involvement of the community and voluntary sector, but rarely will there be the resources, time-scale and understanding of the means that will encourage community participation. Nothing better illustrates this than the 1992 City Challenge bids to the Department of the Environment from local authorities. In an analysis of the bid documents, a CDF report concludes (CDF, 1992):

'the same terms keep creeping up: 'empowerment'; 'capacity-building'; 'active citizenship'; 'developing a sense of place'… These are all important goals, but their repetitive deployment would be more convincing if more than a handful of the bid documents gave any indication of the *means* by which they might be achieved. The abiding impression is … of goals being treated as means; if one chants 'capacity building' often enough, like a mantra, the community will become empowered ... few bids give more than a passing nod to the concept of community development ... There is little evidence of any recognition of the barriers ... which prevent community development, and which demand a clear support and development programme if they are to be overcome.'

Yet when I recently asked a group of CDF staff to list what they saw as the achievements of community development over the past 25 years, they provided a very up-beat assessment. The major achievements that attracted a considerable degree of consensus were as follows.

Fostering a sense of complexity

Community development has made policy-makers more aware of the linkages in effective programmes for regeneration; between, for instance, economic and social factors. There is also more acceptance that success in, for example, crime prevention or social care strategies requires healthy local networks amongst people and groups. Linked to this, there is now greater awareness that need is rarely divisible, and therefore of the value of cross sector and inter-agency initiatives which are community-based.

Reaching the hardest to reach

There is now a considerable number of occupations which have successfully used community development to deliver their services to those population groups most in need, but least accessible to conventional ways of reaching them.

Positive action and equal opportunities

Community development has made a major practical contribution to helping women, black communities and a number of relatively powerless groups to be more assertive and better organised at local level.

Organising the community sector

There has been a substantial growth in the number of local civic, environmental, social and economic groups, much of which was stimulated by the methods and resources of community development. There has therefore been a major contribution to building up the local community sector, and identifying its distinctive contribution in public life.

Getting people involved

From Skeffington (1969) onwards, through consumerism, active citizenship and the citizen's charter, community development's 'great contribution' has been its influence on programmes of public participation, from planning to tenant participation, and consumer and user involvement in, for example, health and social welfare services. Promoting participation has become an accepted element of good practice in public authorities' relationships with their citizens. Community development has shown that service users can engage with providers to make services more innovative, effective, economic and relevant, and it has helped to persuade providers to become more user-friendly, open and accountable.

Extending the meaning of regeneration

There is greater awareness that effective regeneration requires attention to more than narrow economic or environmental initiatives. Community development has helped in two specific ways: it has shown, first, how 'a sense of confidence, identity and ownership amongst local people' forms a basic ingredient for effective regeneration (CDF, 1994a); and, second, how resident-driven community enterprise can play a part alongside macro-economic investment, and act as a bridge to mainstream economic activity. Recognition is also growing of the added value provided by the voluntary action of local residents working together to improve the facilities of their locality.

Ordinary but effective

Community development has demonstrated that 'ordinary' people, and often those with little in the way of power and self-confidence, can take and hold power responsibly to run organisations that will improve neighbourhood life. Community development has also provided workable alternatives to the failure of the private and public sectors to deal effectively with poverty and disadvantage. Credit unions, food co-ops, community businesses and community housing associations have shown that there is another way.

In my view, community development has played a significant part in what the Barclay report (1983) called 'a very general movement away from centralism and towards a belief in ordinary people.' In the late 1960s and for much of the next decade, too, it was invariably community workers who developed the capacity of 'ordinary people' to challenge the local authority, and particularly those responsible for insensitive decisions in housing redevelopment, planning and architecture. In the 1980s, the effect of community development was felt more directly within public authorities, as many sought to implement programmes of decentralisation, and of user participation in the design and delivery of services. There was increasing recognition, too, that authorities should try to strengthen voluntary and neighbourhood initiatives, rather than being obstructive or patronising. This link between the grass-roots actions of the 1970s and the more top-down changes in attitudes and structures of the 1980s is at the centre of community development's contribution to public service. The link is at its most evident and concrete, for example, in the connection between the tenants' battles of the late 1960s and early 1970s (often just to get a decent repair service) and the widespread acceptance today of the need for tenant participation in housing management.

There are two ironies at the heart of the achievements of community development. The first is that what has been practised in the UK has largely been an incomplete version of community development, lacking both intellectual and practical attention to sustaining the kinds of social processes described in section 3.

The second is that the values and methods of community development have been widely diffused, but it itself is hardly visible and understood. Community development has found obscurity in accomplishment; in the successful diffusion of its ideas, it has experienced the dissipation of its own identity.

References

Allinson, C. (1978) *Young Volunteers?* (London: Community Development Foundation)

Barclay, P. Chair, (1982) *Social Workers: Their Roles and Tasks* (London: Bedford Square Press)

Barton, A.H. (1969) *Communities in Disaster: A Sociological Analysis of Collective Stress Situations* (London: Ward Lock)

Bell, J. (1992) *Community Development Teamwork: Measuring the Impact* (London: Community Development Foundation)

—— (1993) 'The Activist and the Alienated', paper, Spring Research Forum, San Antonio, Texas

Blewitt, H. and Garratt, C. (1993) *Tenant Participation in Housing Associations* (London: Community Development Foundation)

—— (1995) *Making It Work* (London: Community Development Foundation)

Boyle, E., Chair, (1973) *Current Issues in Community Work* (London: Routledge & Kegan Paul)

Butcher, H. et al (1993) *Community and Public Policy* (London: Pluto Press/Community Development Foundation/Bradford and Ilkley Community College)

Chanan, G. (1992) *Out of the Shadows* (Dublin: European Foundation for the Improvement of Living and Working Conditions) with a summary, (1994) *Discovering Community Action* (London: Community Development Foundation)

Community Development Foundation (1992) *Mind the Gap: The Community in City Challenge* (London: Community Development Foundation)

Community Development Foundation (1994) 'Foundations for the Future: An Evaluation of the Ogwr Valleys Team' (London: Community Development Foundation, unpublished)

Community Development Foundation (1994a) *Community Involvement in Urban Regeneration*, mimeo (London: Community Development Foundation)

Community Projects Foundation (1982) *Community Development: The Work of the Community Projects Foundation* (London: Community Projects Foundation)

Fisker, J. (1992) *Experiments as a Strategy for Change?* (Copenhagen: AKF Forlaget)

Francis, D. et al (1984) *A Survey of Community Workers in the UK* (London: National Institute of Social Work)

Francis, D. and Henderson, P. (1992) *Working with Rural Communities* (London: Macmillan Books)

—— (1994) *Community Development and Rural Issues* (London: Community Development Foundation/ACRE)

Henderson, P. and Francis, D. (1993) *Rural Action* (London: Pluto Press/Community Development Foundation/ACRE)

Goodenough, W.H. (1963) *Cooperation in Change: An Anthropological Approach to Community Development* (New York: Russell Sage)

Jacobs, J. (1972) *The Life and Death of Great American Cities* (Harmondsworth: Penguin Books)

Jones, D. et.al. (1980) *The Boundaries of Change in Community Work* (London: Allen and Unwin)

Key, M et al. (1976) *Evaluation Theory and Community Work* (London: Community Projects Foundation)

Rumbles, P. (1990) *Selfstart in Business* (London: Community Projects Foundation)

Saunders, P. (1986) *Social Theory and the Urban Question* (London: Hutchinson)

Schoenberg, S.P. and Rosenbaum, P.L. (1980) *Neighbourhoods that Work: Sources for Viability in the Inner City* (New Brunswick, New Jersey: Rutgers University Press)

Seebohm, F. Chair (1968) *Report of the Committee on Local Authority and Allied Personal Social Services* (London: HMSO)

Skeffington, A.M., Chair (1969) *People and Planning* (London; HMSO)

Smith, J. (1992) *Tenant Participation in Housing Organisations* (London: Community Development Foundation)

Thomas, D.N. (1983) *The Making of Community Work* (London: Allen and Unwin)

—— (1995 forthcoming) *Uses and Abuses in Community Development: Essays from the Work of Community Development Foundation* (London: Community Development Foundation)

Willmott, P. (1989) *Community Initiatives* (London: Policy Studies Institute)

Younghusband, E., Chair (1968) *Community Work and Social Change* (London: Longmans)